10651346

10 January 2019

We are lovebirds
and sweethearts

Let's read one every night
together

Happy Birthday + Love
Ellie xo

LOVEBIRDS

AND OTHER WILD SWEETHEARTS

An Hachette UK Company
www.hachette.co.uk

First published in Great Britain in 2019 by Ilex, an imprint of
Octopus Publishing Group Ltd
Carmelite House
50 Victoria Embankment
London EC4Y 0DZ
www.octopusbooks.co.uk
www.octopusbooksusa.com

Design, layout and text copyright © Octopus Publishing Group Ltd 2019
Illustrations copyright © Liz Temperley 2019
Illustration on cover and page 79: 'Mr + Mrs' by Liz Temperley © Liz Temperley 2019
Text by Abbie Headon

Distributed in the US by
Hachette Book Group
1290 Avenue of the Americas
4th and 5th Floors
New York, NY 10104

Distributed in Canada by
Canadian Manda Group
664 Annette St.
Toronto, Ontario, Canada M6S 2C8

Publisher: Alison Starling
Editorial Director: Helen Rochester
Commissioning Editor: Zara Anvari
Managing Editor: Frank Gallaugher
Editor: Jenny Dye
Publishing Assistant: Stephanie Hetherington
Art Director: Julie Weir
Designer: Megan van Staden
Production Manager: Caroline Alberti

All rights reserved. No part of this work may be reproduced or utilised in any form
or by any means, electronic or mechanical, including photocopying, recording or by
any information storage and retrieval system, without the prior written permission
of the publisher.

Abbie Headon and Liz Temperley have asserted their right under the Copyright,
Designs and Patents Act 1988 to be identified as the authors of this work.

ISBN 978-1-78157-621-2

A CIP catalogue record for this book is available from the British Library.

Printed and bound in China

10 9 8 7 6 5 4 3 2 1

LOVEBIRDS

AND OTHER WILD SWEETHEARTS

LIZ TEMPERLEY

INTRODUCTION

Love makes the world go round. It can
work wonders, putting smiles on people's faces
and keeping our relationships together even when
times get tough. However, love is not always easy.

Whether you are wooing a new love or nurturing
an old one, you can find the answer to any romantic
dilemma in the skies, forests and seas. Follow the
example of wild sweethearts who know with
their deepest instincts that they've found
a partner for life.

Some animals sing and dance together to
build a relationship, while others give gifts.
For certain creatures, shared feeding and grooming
strengthens their bonds, and for many, building
a home together is a project that creates
a lasting emotional connection.

The natural world is full of creatures whose
wisdom we can learn from. So let's meet
the couples of the animal kingdom that
really understand the magic of love.

BARN OWL

When you fall for someone, your first challenge is to attract their attention and show them you're worth a second look. The courtship of barn owls begins with swoops and romantic screeches, and later on the male will provide gifts of food to his mate, while she sits and preens. In this way, they start a relationship that will last a lifetime.

GREATER FLAMINGO

Entering the dating world can be daunting
on your own – so why not go out with a squad
of friends instead? When flamingos are in the
mood for love, they put on a synchronised dancing
display in groups of fifteen or more, all in an
attempt to attract the perfect mate.

EURASIAN MAGPIE

Love is transformational, turning
even the gruffest of us into true romantics.
When the mating season arrives, male magpies
swap their harsh barking chatter for soft seductive
calls, accompanied by flight displays and feather-
fanning. By revealing their gentler side, these
tough guys of the bird world show they're
ready to settle down.

C O Y O T E

Life doesn't always provide a whirlwind
romance: sometimes love is a waiting game.
When coyotes are courting, a female will often
keep her distance and appear to be uninterested.
But if the male gives her space and shows
respect, the pair can form a lifelong bond.

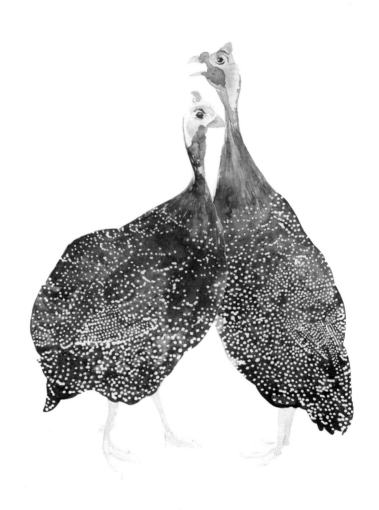

GUINEA FOWL

What's the best way to show you're an ideal partner? If you're a male guinea fowl, the answer is to take part in a race with all the other young males in your flock. Through this athletic display, these birds attract partners by demonstrating an ability to protect their families effectively.

ATLANTIC PUFFIN

However hectic our lives are, it's our simple
shared rituals that bring us together. These
clown-faced birds express their feelings by
wagging their heads from side to side and
rattling their beaks together, both during
courtship and throughout their lives.

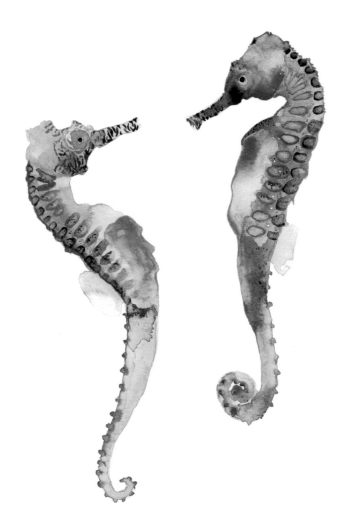

TIGER-SNOUT SEAHORSE

We often try to look our best when
we're feeling romantic, with a smart jacket
or an elegant dress. When these tiny seahorses
court, they put on their own display of finery
by changing their body colour and swimming
in synchrony over several days.

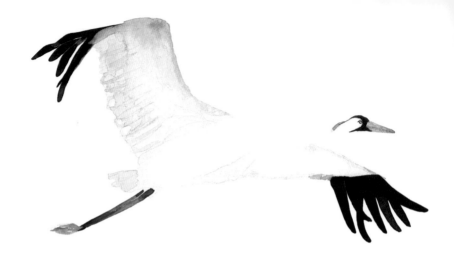

WHOOPING CRANE

Dancing adds joy to any romance. At mating time, one crane will invite another to dance by tossing its head and stamping its feet. Birds display their mutual attraction and build trust by copying each other's movements in a stunning ballet of leaping and head-bobbing.

SCARLET MACAW

It's important to think carefully about what
you want from a relationship before committing.
These colourful parrots take great care when
choosing a mate, knowing that they'll be doing
almost everything together for the rest of their
lives. Occasionally a scarlet macaw will play
house with two partners before settling
down with 'the one'.

BALD EAGLE

Showing that you trust one another in risky
situations is one way to deepen a relationship.
While courting, bald eagles will swoop and
dive together in the air, even locking talons
and skydiving, releasing each other just
before they reach they ground.

BALD UAKARI

Beauty is in the eye of the beholder, and to these monkeys there's no sight more enticing than a bright red face, signifying health and vigour. Females release an attractive scent to draw males towards them, in just the same way that we splash on our favourite perfume before a date.

VICTORIA CROWNED PIGEON

Why be plain when you can be extraordinary?
That's the rule these giant and extravagant
pigeons live by, with their matching frilly crests
and stunning blue plumage. When you find
someone who shares your quirky style, it could
be a sign that you are meant to be together.

SUN PARAKEET

These vibrantly coloured birds express
their love by feeding and grooming each other.
Through small acts of intimacy, their relationship
bonds grow stronger, as each partner shows
their commitment and trust.

GREAT HORNBILL

When you're in love, you want the whole
world to know about it. Great hornbills sing
loud duets during courtship, showing everyone
around them that they're together. This bond
will serve them well when the female is raising
their chicks inside a hollow tree, relying
on her mate to provide food.

BLACK VULTURE

We all have our own idea of romance. Black vultures can't sing, so they express their feelings through grunts and hisses. Instead of building a nest, they decorate the area where they'll lay their eggs with bottle tops and pieces of plastic.

EURASIAN BEAVER

You need patience and a positive attitude if you're going to succeed in love, as these Eurasian beavers prove. The female beaver is only ready to conceive a new litter on one day of each year, so she and her mate have to be ready to seize the moment when it comes!

LONG-FINNED GOBY

When we each play to our strengths, we can celebrate our differences and achieve our shared goals. In sunny lagoons, these gobies divide their work in just this way: the female builds a burrow, and the male watches over it and tends to their eggs.

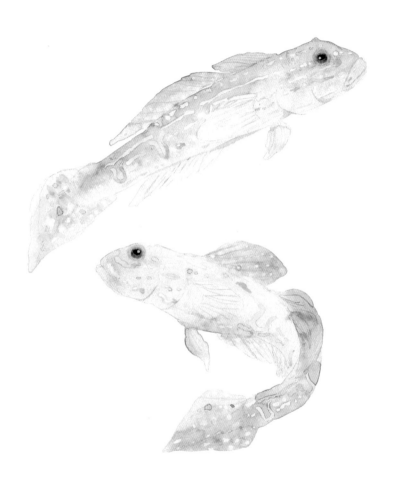

AZARA'S NIGHT MONKEY

These tree-dwelling monkeys know how to share the work of parenthood. After the first week, the father takes over all the responsibility of carrying their little one for the next four to five months. This helps the mother maintain her energy levels for feeding, and keeps the whole family safe.

ANTAPcTIc PPION

Spending half the year swooping over
the oceans and the other half nesting with
their partners, Antarctic prions have found the
perfect balance of freedom and home-making.
We all need to stretch our wings sometimes,
but there's no place like home.

MACARONI PENGUIN

Teamwork is the bedrock of every good
relationship. Each pair of macaroni penguins
begins by looking after their new egg together.
After twelve days, the male leaves to forage
for food, returning twelve days later so
that the female can go and eat.

LAYSAN ALBATROSS

Love's magic is waiting to happen to all
of us, and isn't determined by our age, gender
or any other factor. Although Laysan albatrosses
usually form male-female pairs, in some colonies
pairs of two females are found successfully
raising families together. We can learn
a lot from Nature's example.

ANDEAN CONDOR

These majestic birds form a pair bond that can last for fifty years or more. From their nest high on a rocky crag, they work together to raise and protect their family. However windswept and rugged their homes are, their relationship is strong enough to weather any storm.

HARLEQUIN SHRIMP

Attitude can make a big difference. These tiny
shrimps aren't afraid to tackle creatures ten
or twenty times bigger than they are when
out hunting for food. By working together,
couples ensure that they have enough
food to survive and raise a family.

MUTE SWAN

When you're in love, protecting your partner
and offspring is a natural instinct. Mute swans
are vigilant in keeping danger at bay, but before
resorting to a physical attack, they will start
by giving a loud hiss, to say 'stay away!'
This tactic allows peace to be restored
with only a few ruffled feathers.

PRAIRIE VOLE

The world can be a scary place when you're small enough to live in someone's pocket, but with a partner by your side, nothing seems too daunting. These little furry creatures express affection and strengthen their lifelong bond by snuggling together and grooming one another.

D I K - D I K

These gentle-eyed creatures understand
how important it is to spend time together.
Pairs of male and female dik-diks can usually
be found close to one another, providing
companionship and security for each other
through all of life's ups and downs.

BLUE JAY

Nobody knows what the future has in store, and
it's wise to prepare ourselves for challenging
times. Just as we save for a rainy day, pairs of
blue jays work hard together to collect and
store nuts and acorns, ready to return
to in the harsh days of winter.

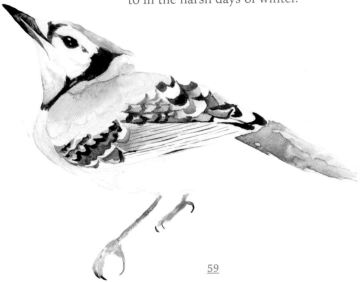

SPECTRAL BAT

When love overwhelms us, we want to wrap our partner in this glorious emotion, keeping them safe from any danger outside. That's precisely what a male spectral bat will do: when sleeping, he will often shelter his partner and their offspring by snuggling them up inside his wings.

RED-TAILED HAWK

Love will find a way, despite all difficulties
and obstacles. Red-tailed hawks usually live in
forests and fields, but some determined pairs
make their homes on city skyscrapers. Despite
the dangers of crashing into windows, eating
poisoned food or being harassed by humans,
their love enables them to keep going.

FRENCH ANGELFISH

These brightly coloured fish can usually be
found swimming together in pairs. When the
time comes to breed, they swim slowly upwards,
releasing their sperm and eggs closely together.
Their bond is formed by the need to protect
their larvae from dangerous predators
lurking in the coral reef.

GRAY WOLF

Strong relationships are based on daily acts of kindness as well as the bigger gestures such as giving gifts. After giving birth, a mother wolf stays in her den for a few weeks looking after her cubs, and her partner brings her the food she needs to stay strong and healthy.

SEA OTTER

What's more reassuring than knowing that
your partner is close to you while you sleep?
Sea otter pairs hold hands in the water while
they rest, to ensure that they won't drift apart
and wake alone. Dreams are always sweeter
when the one you love is near.

BLACK - BACKED JACKAL

Communication is a vital element of lasting
relationships. Pairs of jackals yelp, whine,
growl and bark together to spread messages
to their family group and tell the world
about their territory. It's good to talk.

CALIFORNIA MOUSE

We know it's better to make love, not war.
Male California mice spend time defending
their territories by jumping and squeaking, but
they have to balance this against the need to care
for their families. Focusing on a more peaceful
life gives us more time to spend with our
loved ones, on things that really matter.

SHINGLEBACK
SKINK

Appearances can be deceptive: although these
skinks are covered in armour-plating, underneath
their rugged exterior they are as soft-hearted as
the next romantic. Once they have formed a pair,
they have been known to return to one another
to breed for as long as twenty years.

GOLDEN EAGLE

Cooperation is very important in relationships
that last. These mighty predators work alongside
one another in nest-building and hunting for food,
and they can stay together for their whole lives.
While courting, a pair of eagles will perform aerial
displays of dropping and catching items, showing
off the skills they will use in their lives together.

ROSY-FACED LOVEBIRD

Some partners, just like these lovebirds,
are so alike that it's hard to tell them apart.
Once bonded, they stay together for the rest
of their lives, feeding and grooming each other,
and sleeping with their faces turned in towards
one another. When separated, they pine for
their mate, just like humans do.

TURTLE DOVE

These gentle birds use their distinctive
purring song to attract a mate, and have inspired
poets, writers and artists for centuries with their
example of lifelong love. Shakespeare called on
the turtle dove in his poem 'The Phoenix and the
Turtle', and the English folk song 'Ten Thousand
Miles' compares the singer's love to the
turtle dove's faithfulness.

GRAY FOX

Gray foxes are able to climb trees just as cats do, which means they can snuggle down for a nap together high up in the branches. Finding space for shared moments of calm is an important way to stay in touch with one another and build a long-lasting relationship.

BLACK AND RUFOUS ELEPHANT SHREW

Some couples feel most relaxed when they give each other plenty of space. These long-nosed shrews bond for life, working together to defend a large territory and raise their young, but they like to spend most of their time apart.

GIBBON

Love can be thrilling, making you want
to celebrate with everyone around. When
gibbons strike up a duet, their love song can
be heard half a mile away. They know that love
is too precious to be hidden, and only
grows from being shared.

SOUTHERN ROCKHOPPER PENGUIN

They say that absence makes the heart
grow fonder, and this is certainly true for these
punky-feathered seabirds. Although they spend
almost all year swimming hundreds of miles
apart, year after year when it's time to mate,
a pair of rockhoppers will find one another,
drawn together by the mystery of love.

CANADA GOOSE

Some of these boisterous birds migrate
thousands of miles as the seasons change,
while others are content to live all year round in
the same city park. Whether you are explorers
or homebodies, experiencing the world
together makes life an adventure.

MALAGASY GIANT RAT

We all need a special place where we
feel safe and snug. For these large rodents
from Madasgascar, home sweet home is an
underground burrow several feet wide.
They spend every day together in the burrow
before venturing out to find food in the
peace and quiet of the night.

WESTERN OSPREY

Sometimes you understand how much you truly
love someone when you're away from them –
and there's nothing better than the joy of being
reunited. Ospreys migrate thousands of miles
every summer and winter, and when their long
journey is over, they find their life partner and
begin the joyful work of nesting once again.

ACKNOWLEDGEMENTS

For my Mum and Matt: here's a silver
lining for you. Thank you for the support,
always, Katy and Russ. And Haydn,
thank you from the start x

Thank you to Alice for being
a superstar expert friend.

And a big thank you to Zara and the team
at Octopus for giving me the opportunity
to work on such a lovely lovely project!